YOU CHOOSE

CAN YOU ESCAPE A HAUNTED CASTLE?

AN INTERACTIVE PARANORMAL ADVENTURE

BY AILYN

CAPSTONE PRESS
a capstone imprint

Published by Capstone Press, an imprint of Capstone
1710 Roe Crest Drive, North Mankato, Minnesota 56003
capstonepub.com

Copyright © 2025 by Capstone. All rights reserved. No part of this publication may be reproduced in whole or in part, or stored in a retrieval system, or transmitted in any form or by any means, electronic, mechanical, photocopying, recording, or otherwise, without written permission of the publisher.

Library of Congress Cataloging-in-Publication Data

Names: Collins, Ailynn, 1964- author. Title: Can you escape a haunted castle? : an interactive paranormal adventure / by Ailynn Collins.
Description: North Mankato, Minnesota : Capstone Press, an imprint of Capstone, 2024. | Series: You choose: haunted adventures | Includes bibliographical references. | Audience: Ages 8 to 12. | Audience: Grades 4-6.
Summary: An interactive adventure where the reader explores haunted castles around the world in search of paranormal activity for a school report. Includes additional information about famous castle hauntings.
Identifiers: LCCN 2024005436 (print) | LCCN 2024005437 (ebook) | ISBN 9781669069089 (hardcover) | ISBN 9781669069058 (paperback) | ISBN 9781669069065 (pdf) | ISBN 9781669069072 (epub)
Subjects: CYAC: Haunted places--Fiction. | Castles--Fiction. | Plot-your-own stories. | LCGFT: Choose-your-own stories.
Classification: LCC PZ7.1.P456 Cao 2024 (print) | LCC PZ7.1.P456 (ebook) | DDC [Fic]--dc23
LC record available at https://lccn.loc.gov/2024005436
LC ebook record available at https://lccn.loc.gov/2024005437

Editorial Credits
Editor: Mandy Robbins; Designer: Dina Her; Media Researcher: Jo Miller; Production Specialist: Tori Abraham

Photo Credits
Alamy: dpa picture alliance, 34; Getty Images: Yevgeniy Kharitonov, 23; Shutterstock: Azston Designs, 102, BLACKDAY, 66, clearlens, 40, Dennis Diatel, 95, Derick P. Hudson, 10, drasa, 27, Eric Isselee, 78, f4 Luftbilder, 37, FOTOKITA, 45, Kelleher Photography, 21, 30, LaineN, 93, Lucian BOLCA, 106, Marti Bug Catcher, 81, Melinda Nagy, 14, Nikki Gensert, 33, Pelevina Ksinia, 60, pratilop prombud, Cover (moon), Raggedstone, 105, Sean Pavone, 72, Sola Solandra, Cover (castle), superjoseph, 75, zef art, 53

Design Elements
Shutterstock: Nik Merkulov, Olha Nion

Any additional websites and resources referenced in this book are not maintained, authorized, or sponsored by Capstone. All product and company names are trademarks™ or registered® trademarks of their respective holders.

Printed and bound in China. 6274

TABLE OF CONTENTS

INTRODUCTION
ABOUT YOUR ADVENTURE................5

CHAPTER 1
A DIFFICULT CHOICE....................7

CHAPTER 2
LEAP CASTLE IN IRELAND..............11

CHAPTER 3
CASTLE FRANKENSTEIN
IN ODENWALD, GERMANY 35

CHAPTER 4
THE FORBIDDEN CITY IN BEIJING, CHINA 73

CHAPTER 5
ARE CASTLE HAUNTINGS REAL?..........103

MORE GHOSTLY ENCOUNTERS 106
OTHER PATHS TO EXPLORE 108
GLOSSARY.............................109
BIBLIOGRAPHY 110
READ MORE............................111
INTERNET SITES.......................111
ABOUT THE AUTHOR 112

INTRODUCTION
ABOUT YOUR ADVENTURE

YOU are doing research for a school project on haunted castles around the world. What you are learning gives you chills. Watching online videos about people's paranormal experiences makes you wonder if perhaps ghosts just might be real. What would you do if you encountered a spirit in a haunted castle?

Chapter One sets the scene. Then you choose which path to read. Follow the directions at the bottom of the page as you read the stories. The decisions you make will change your outcome. After you finish one path, go back and read the others for new perspectives and more adventures.

Turn the page to begin your adventure.

CHAPTER 1
A DIFFICULT CHOICE

For your project, you've focused on three castles. Leap Castle in Ireland, Castle Frankenstein in Germany, and the Forbidden City in China have gripped your imagination.

Leap Castle is one of the most haunted places in the world. Many visitors have reported strange experiences there. Castle Frankenstein inspired the book *Frankenstein* by Mary Shelley. Your aunt Sharon lives near it. And your grandma has told you many spooky stories about the Forbidden City, a palace in Beijing. That's where she grew up.

Turn the page.

There is a school trip to Beijing over spring break. You want to go, but you are afraid to ask for the money. Then your dad surprises you.

"Your research on haunted castles has given me an idea," he says. "Do you want to visit one this year? If you pick Ireland, we'll go in the summer. If you pick China, we'll pay for your school trip."

"If you choose Germany, we should go around Halloween," adds Mom. "Sharon says that's the best time to visit Castle Frankenstein."

Where will you choose? Would you like to go with your friends to China or with your family to Germany or Ireland?

- To choose Leap Castle, turn to page 11.
- To choose Castle Frankenstein, turn to page 35.
- To choose the Forbidden City, turn to page 73.

CHAPTER 2
LEAP CASTLE IN IRELAND

You can't pass up a trip to Ireland and Leap Castle. Its history is full of murder and bloody clan warfare. You hope for a ghostly encounter.

When you arrive at the castle, you and your parents walk along a path by a crumbled wall. At the end stands the grey, stone castle. It's not as big as you imagined, but something about it makes you shiver. The castle is rumored to have a torture pit beneath it. Tortured spirits may not have found the peace needed to move on to the afterlife.

Turn the page.

The owner greets you inside. "Welcome," he says, "This is the Great Hall. Feel free to walk around the castle. I've owned it since 1991. I've fixed up some parts, but the spirits don't seem to want me to finish—a couple nasty accidents while working. Other than that, the spirits haven't harmed me. Beware of the Elemental, though. I haven't seen it, but legend says it is powerful and evil."

"Wasn't it put here to protect this place by the Druids?" you ask. You had learned about the Elemental in your research.

The man nods, impressed by your knowledge. "Possibly. Some say it was made from Druid magic. Others say it was placed here by the Earl of Kildare. Either way, the Elemental may push you out of some rooms. Don't challenge him."

You nod nervously and walk through the Great Hall. The castle is decorated with artifacts and art. Old furniture crowds the space, and plants grow freely about many of the stone walls. It's smaller than you expected, but there is so much to see in all of its nooks and crannies. A narrow stone staircase behind a wooden door leads to the second floor.

"If we get separated, meet back here," Dad says.

You wander about, and your parents follow behind. You zip up your jacket. It's suddenly chilly.

Then you hear giggling. You turn toward the sound and squint. You see two young girls in long dresses playing. They wave you over, and you smile. Before you can move toward them, a woman in a black dress appears out of nowhere. She steps between you and the girls, scowling.

Turn the page.

You fall back, bumping into your dad. All three figures flicker away in the sunlight streaming through a window.

"Did you see that?" you ask him.

"See what?" he asks.

"Never mind," you say, trying to convince yourself you were imagining the girls and the woman. Your parents turn to leave, but before you follow them, one of the little girls reappears. She beckons you around a corner and then disappears behind it.

"Let's go to up to the Bloody Chapel," Mom says, nervously.

"OK," you say, but you're not really paying attention.

You're still curious about those little girls. Part of you really wants to follow them.

- To follow the girls, turn to page 16.
- To follow your parents to the Chapel, turn to page 29.

You can't help but follow the girls. Around the corner is a narrow stone hall. The girls are gone. There's very little light, and cobwebs hang down like curtains. You're about to turn back when you hear giggling again. You squeeze down the hallway. You're sure the girls are just around the next corner.

The hall bends to the right and ends at another doorway. You look in and see two crumbling stone platforms amidst the dust and cobwebs. When you blink, the slabs become two small beds. An old cradle sits in one corner.

Suddenly, you hear a sob and look up. A woman in a red dress holds a knife over you. Her face is streaked with tears. She's about to bring down the knife on you! You scream and cower in the other end of the small room. The red lady blocks your way out.

You hide behind the old cradle. But the lady keeps slashing the knife at you, missing your head by inches.

The two girls suddenly appear in the other corner of the room. Their giggles distract the red lady. You take advantage and dash to the door. As you look back, the room is dark and empty again.

What just happened? You don't stop to think about it. You have to tell your parents what happened. Where did they say they were going? The Upper Hall or the Bloody Chapel? The Upper Hall is on the second floor. The Bloody Chapel is on the third.

- To go to the Upper Hall, turn to page 18.
- To go to the Bloody Chapel, turn to page 21.

It seems logical that they would go to the second floor before they go to the third floor. You climb the stairs to the second floor and push open a large, heavy door. You are greeted with an icy breeze, even though the windows are closed.

The room holds a dining table and some other old furniture. The decor is fascinating, with old painting, stuffed birds, and old oil lamps. An antique rug covers the floor. There's a strange stain on one end of the floor, but you chalk it up to the castle being so old.

You don't see Mom or Dad, but a young man stands by a window, looking at the gardens outside. Maybe he has seen them.

"Excuse me," you say, worrying you've disturbed him.

"Tell me why," he says, staring out the window. His voice echoes.

"Why what?" you ask, noticing the man's strange outfit. It's as if he was getting into medieval armor but stopped halfway. Chain mail hangs off of him.

"Why did he kill us?" he asks sadly.

You stop in your tracks. Is this a reenactor, or ghost? You can't be sure.

The man turns to face you. His eyes flash in anger. Suddenly, he rises off the ground and floats toward you. He must be another spirit! Before you can even think, he dissolves into a large white cloud that whooshes right through you.

It feels like being hit by a giant snowball. You are slammed against a wall. The last thing you remember is sliding down onto the floor before everything goes black.

Turn the page.

When your eyes open, you see sunshine. You're lying on the front lawn. Mom and Dad stand over you, worried. The old owner has a smirk on his face.

"I told you to be careful," he says.

"What happened?" Mom asks.

You don't know what happened or how you got here, and you don't want to talk about it. All you can do is cry.

"Can we go, please?" you whimper.

Your parents take you back to the hotel. They keep asking you what happened. But the thought of what you saw and the question of how you ended up outside scares you too much.

THE END

To follow another path, turn to page 8.
To learn more about haunted castles, turn to page 103.

You're pretty sure your parents were going to the Bloody Chapel. You slog up the narrow, spiral staircase. There's no electricity. Some sections are so dark, you can barely see.

You peek in the Upper Hall on the second floor and are hit with an awful smell. You see a dark stain on the floor. It's about the size of a watermelon. It's odd, but you keep climbing.

The Upper Hall

Turn the page.

Finally, you reach the third floor. When you push open the heavy, wooden door, the room is so bright, you can barely look inside. Out of the corner of your eye, you see the same stain on the floor. A chill runs through you. Can a stain follow you?

You're a bit shaken up and ready to run back down to the Great Hall. Just as you turn to go, a blood-curdling scream fills the air. It sounds like Mom. Is she in the chapel?

- To go down to the Great Hall, go to the next page.
- To look for Mom in the chapel, turn to page 25.

Mom must be safe with Dad. You have to get out of this place. You stumble down the staircase. Your hands shove open the wooden door into the Great Hall. The owner gives you a surprised look as you run outside. You find yourself back in the sunny garden. Everything feels normal out here.

Shaking, you sit on a low stone wall and wait for your parents to come out. When they do, they look worried.

Turn the page.

"Why didn't you meet us by the stairs? We were worried," Dad asks.

"I forgot," you lie. "Did you see anything unusual?"

They shake their heads. "It was an interesting castle with lots of history," Mom says.

"I'm disappointed we didn't see any ghosts," Dad says. "How was your experience?"

You're never going to tell them what you experienced there. They wouldn't believe you anyway.

"Let's just explore Ireland," you say. "I've had enough of castles for a while."

THE END

To follow another path, turn to page 8.
To learn more about haunted castles, turn to page 103.

The scream really sounded like Mom. You can't ignore it. You gather your courage and step into the Bloody Chapel. Either your eyes have adjusted to the sunlight, or the lighting has dimmed. The room is nothing but crumbling stone and birds' nests. The windows have no glass. There is an odd hole in one corner of the room. It creeps you out.

You're about to turn back when you hear a whimper.

"Mom?" you ask.

There is no answer. Could she have slipped down that hole? You nervously look into it, but you don't see anything but birds' nests.

"Mom?" you call.

Turn the page.

You step toward the hole and your body gets weak. An invisible force punches you in the stomach. You catch yourself before falling down the hole. You scramble to your feet and run to the door. That's when you come face-to-face with the scariest thing you've ever seen.

It's grey and see-through. Two large black eyes stare at you. Its mouth is long and thin. This creature feels like pure evil.

You want to scream, but nothing comes out of your mouth. You can't breathe. Your vision fills with black spots. Just as the ghostly creature is about to overwhelm you, everything around you goes black.

When you wake up, you're lying on a couch in the Great Hall. You hear your parents and the owner speaking. You open your eyes and sit up.

Turn the page.

"What happened?" Mom asks. "A tourist found you passed out in the Bloody Chapel."

"He said something about the Elemental," Dad adds.

"Fascinating," the owner says. "Legend has it that the wife of the last lord to live here, Mildred Darby, meddled with spirits and awakened the Elemental. I've never seen it, though."

You shiver again. "Can we leave?" You ask your parents. You never thought you'd say this, but you've had enough of haunted places.

THE END

To follow another path, turn to page 8.
To learn more about haunted castles, turn to page 103.

Whatever it was you saw has you spooked. You decide to stick with your parents. You follow them up a dark, winding staircase to the top of the tower. A doorway leads into what is known as the Bloody Chapel.

When you reach it, there's a group of tourists inside. Someone is telling a story of the O'Carroll family. They fought battles in the 1500s to keep control of this castle.

"In 1532, the chieftain was Mulroney O'Carroll. When he died, his sons fought over the property. One was a priest. He is said to have held a mass for the family without telling his brother. This was considered a terrible insult. His brother entered the chapel and ran a sword through the priest. The priest died on the altar. This is why it's called the "Bloody Chapel," she explains.

Turn the page.

A window in the Bloody Chapel

The guide moves over to another section of the room that has a small hole in the floor.

"This chapel had a trap door in the floor that opened to a small but frightening room," she says, "Prisoners were pushed down this hole. When they landed in the room below, they might be pierced by spikes and die. If they didn't, they would starve to death."

The group then leaves the chapel. Dad and Mom go to the windows and admire the view. You look down the hole. You think you hear the echoes of screams. It makes you shiver.

"Do you hear that?" you ask your parents.

They don't answer. Their gaze is fixed on the view. They look frozen in place.

Turn the page.

The room is suddenly cold. The screams grow louder. From the bottom of the hole, you hear cries for help. You flatten yourself on the floor against the edge of the hole.

"Is there someone there?" you call down.

"He killed us all," an eerie voice says.

Suddenly, a strong gust of wind whooshes out of the hole into the room. You look up at the ceiling. There, looking down at you, is the ghost of a medieval soldier. As soon as his eyes lock with yours, he whooshes toward you with an ever-widening mouth. Suddenly, everything goes black.

When you open your eyes again, your parents stand over you.

"Did you fall down?" Mom asks.

"You were frozen," you say.

"What?" Dad sounds puzzled. "We were looking out the window. When we turned around you were on the ground."

You don't know how to explain what happened, and you're not sure you want to tell them what you saw. You'd rather forget it.

Leap Castle

THE END

To follow another path, turn to page 8.
To learn more about haunted castles, turn to page 103.

CHAPTER 3
CASTLE FRANKENSTEIN IN ODENWALD, GERMANY

Halloween is your favorite holiday, so of course, you pick Castle Frankenstein. Plus, you get to visit Aunt Sharon. When you email her, she tells you Frankenstein Castle hosts the largest Halloween party in Germany. How perfect!

Turn the page.

On the plane, you read more about the castle. It has existed since the 1200's. The castle's history is full of stories of witches and mad scientists. Legend tells of a fountain of youth hidden on the property. Even today, people gather in the forest around the castle hoping to drink from this fountain and live forever.

You and your parents arrive in Frankfurt, Germany, on Halloween morning.

"Halloween festivities last two weeks at the castle," Sharon says. "There's plenty of spookiness to be had."

As soon as you're settled, you beg Sharon to take you to the castle. It's Halloween night, after all. Your parents are tired, but you're full of energy. Your cousins are too young for tonight's festivities.

"There's a less scary celebration on Sunday. That's better for my little ones," Sharon says. "If you really want to go tonight, I'll take you."

Your parents would rather you all wait and go together on Sunday. Which do you choose?

Castle Frankenstein from above

- To head to the castle tonight, turn to page 38.
- To wait to go on Sunday, turn to page 56.

You want to go tonight. By the time you arrive at the castle, the sun is almost setting. The forest surrounding the castle is dark and eerie, but the castle is lit up. It's full of people and activity.

You and Sharon walk up a cobblestone path with other partygoers in costumes. You wear a simple black cat costume and Sharon wears vampire fangs. There are spots of fake blood all over her white shirt.

The castle is smaller than you imagined. Parts of the stone walls around the castle are broken or have collapsed.

"It's an old castle," Sharon says. "That's why it's so spooky."

"I hope I see a ghost," you say.

"Careful what you wish for," she warns.

In the courtyard, there's a stage set up. People dressed in medieval costumes act out a scene. A "victim" lies on the floor covered in fake blood. You clap politely when the actors take a bow.

You think you feel a tap on your shoulder. You turn around, but no one's there. Your aunt is several feet away. Someone must have bumped you. But from where you're standing, that seems impossible. You're suddenly uneasy.

You follow Sharon through the crowd. As you reach the other end of the courtyard, you hear a buzzing sound. Your head aches, and everything spins around you. For a moment, everything goes blurry.

When Sharon taps you, it stops. She points to a sign. There's a haunted castle event happening inside.

Turn the page.

"It's pretty scary, especially on Halloween night. Are you sure you want to go in?" she asks.

Do you risk a good scare inside or stay out here?

Castle Frankenstein

- To go inside the haunted castle, go to the next page.
- To stay outside, turn to page 47.

There's a long line to enter the haunted castle. In front of you is a group of teens about your age. They compliment you on your costume and ask you to join them. Sharon seems relieved to leave you with them.

"Find me at the restaurant," she says. "Have fun!"

Your new friends are dressed as witches and wizards. When your group enters, a Frankenstein monster welcomes you. He lets out an evil laugh and pulls back the curtain.

You walk down a dark, crowded hallway. The air is cold. You expect ghouls or monsters to jump out, but they don't. The only sounds you hear are the breaths and footfalls of your group walking through the dark, narrow passageway.

Near the end of the passage, a red light shines. There's a room on your left and another on your right. As you peek into one room, someone jumps out from the other, with a blood-curdling scream. You all jump and scream too.

A mummy with blood oozing from his bandages lumbers at you. Your screams turn to laughter as you avoid the mummy. You enter the room on the left.

It looks like an old laboratory. There's a wooden table with fake body parts laid out on it. They look disturbingly real. A "mad scientist" is sewing a fake body together with a large rusty needle.

"That's supposed to be Johann Konrad Dippel," someone says, pointing to the scientist.

You read about Dippel in your book. He lived during the 1600's. Legend has it that he performed experiments on human bodies.

"They say his ghost still haunts the castle," another friend says.

The actor playing Dippel gives you a bottle of something. "This is Dippel's Oil, my Elixir of Life," he says. "It will cure any illness."

You've read that the real Dippel's elixir was made of blood, leather, horns, and ivory. You open the tiny bottle and pour a drop on your hand. It's dark brown and smells foul.

The room is suddenly empty. Only the body parts remain on the wooden table.

"Hello?" you call out in shock. No one answers. Where did they go?

Turn the page.

You head for the door. It slams shut. You pull the handle, but the door won't budge. You bang on it. Laughter fills the air.

"It's not funny," you say, still banging on the door. Are your new friends playing a trick on you?

Suddenly, the creature on the table moans. Somehow, its limbs have been sewn together. Its eyes blink at you. With one finger it points at the small bottle in your hand, and then at its mouth.

Are these haunted house special effects? They're so real, you're terrified. You play along.

With a shaking hand, you pour a drop of that smelly liquid into the creature's mouth. That seems to wake it up. Its giant hand tries to grab the bottle from you. But when it swipes at you, its hand goes right through yours!

Your heart thumps. That's not possible. You run for the door and pull hard, screaming at the top of your lungs. When it finally opens, you fall onto the stone floor, and everything goes black.

When you wake up, you're lying in bed in a bright room. A nurse looks at you with a frown. She mumbles something and you catch the word "tourist."

Turn the page.

Sharon rushes into the room. "How did you end up in the infirmary?" she gasps. "Are you all right?"

You think about telling her what happened, but she wouldn't believe you. You barely believe it yourself.

"They have some really great special effects," you say as Sharon helps you to your feet.

"Would you like to go home now?" she asks. "We can come back on Sunday, when you feel better."

- To leave and come back Sunday, turn to page 56.
- To stay longer, turn to page 52.

You've only just arrived, but already you're spooked. Maybe you should have waited until Sunday.

But Sharon has driven you an hour to get here, so you should probably stay. Still, you're not quite ready for the haunted house event yet.

"I don't think I want to go inside tonight," you say. You're still trying to figure out why you got so dizzy.

"I'm hungry," Sharon says. "Let's go to the restaurant. Or you can explore and find me there when you're done."

- To go eat with Sharon, turn to page 48.
- To wander the grounds, turn to page 49.

You're hungry too, and you're too spooked to wander on your own. You decide to stick with Sharon. The two of you head to the restaurant and spend the next couple hours catching up and eating delicious food.

"This is actually my second time coming to this event on Halloween," Sharon says. "I wasn't sure I wanted to come back again."

"Why not?" you ask, eagerly.

"You might think I'm crazy, but I saw some things I can't explain," she says.

"I don't," you say. "I've only been here a little while, but whatever you saw, I believe it."

THE END

To follow another path, turn to page 8.
To learn more about haunted castles, turn to page 103.

Bravely, you wander through the courtyard between the castle, the tower, and a small chapel. It's filled with people. Many are dressed in black with tiny skulls hanging off their clothes. Their faces are painted with glowing white paint. Their eyes are lined in black. They even have animal skulls hanging off their tall hairdos. They bump you with every few steps.

"This is what I felt earlier," you tell yourself. "That explains it."

Your head buzzes from the noise, so you move to a quieter spot near the forest. The trees cast long shadows in the moonlight.

As you turn back toward the castle, a young girl runs past you in a white nightgown. She beckons you to follow her. Without thinking, you do.

Soon, you come to a clearing in the trees. A large fire burns in the center. It is surrounded by a ring of girls dressed in white nightgowns. They dance and sing in a language you don't recognize.

You're mesmerized. You have no idea how much time has passed when one of the girls walks over to you. She moves so gracefully she could be floating. In her hand she holds a small, silver cup. She takes a sip, then offers the cup to you. Against your better judgement, you take a sip.

The drink is refreshing and sweet. The forest spins around you. Your ears buzz. You fall to the ground.

When you wake up, you're on a cold, hard bed in a bright room. Sharon is looking down at you.

"What happened?" she asks, with a worried look. "We found you passed out in the chapel."

The chapel? How did you get back there? Your head hurts. You're quite sure you were in the forest. You tell your aunt how you followed the girl to the woods and what you saw.

"It sounds like you found the witches who seek the fountain of youth," a nurse whispers as Sharon gathers up your things. She helps you sit up. "You may live forever now."

You tingle at her words. Only time will tell.

THE END

To follow another path, turn to page 8.
To learn more about haunted castles, turn to page 103.

You and Sharon drove a whole hour to get here. You may be scared, but you're not giving up on this adventure yet.

"Let's explore together," you say to Sharon.

"OK," Sharon says, somewhat reluctantly, "Let's join this group heading to the tower."

You agree. Whatever happens there, at least your aunt won't ditch you like those kids did before.

You climb several flights of stairs. With each level, the air grows colder.

"There's definitely a ghost here," someone says. "My compass isn't working anymore."

You all gather around his compass and see that the needle is spinning fast. You've read that sometimes ghosts can mess with the Earth's electromagnetic field.

At the very top of the tower, you look out at the darkness below. There's a flicker of light in the forest. Are people camping out there tonight?

You turn around to ask, but Aunt Sharon is gone. Not again!

"This isn't funny, Sharon," you call out.

Nervously, you inch back down the stairs. When you get to the second level, you stop to catch your breath. Looking out over the courtyard, you see the rooftop of the chapel.

There's a man sitting on the roof. He's dressed in a medieval costume. In his hand he holds an old wool bag. He's shaking it, rattling whatever is inside. He looks up, and your eyes meet.

He asks you something in German, but you don't understand. You shrug. The man calls out again, louder this time. Then he gets to his feet and jumps off the roof!

Before you can call out to him, he has disappeared into thin air. Your heart leaps into your throat.

"You look like you've seen a ghost!" Sharon says, suddenly at your side.

You tell her about the man who just jumped off the chapel roof.

"That's the ghost of Dippel," she says. "I've heard he's searching for his laboratory. It's buried somewhere underground."

When you get back to the courtyard, some people from your tour group want to go to the forest, the other half want to go into the chapel.

- To go to the forest, turn to page 64.
- To go to the chapel, turn to page 69.

You decide to go on Sunday. Your two little cousins dress up as ghosts. It's more cute than scary, but you are happy the family is going together.

You walk up the cobblestone pathway. The small stone building with crumbling walls is more of a ruin than a castle.

On a stage in a courtyard, actors put on a skit. Your cousins sit in the front row, happy to stay there.

Sharon and your parents are reading the menu outside the castle's restaurant. You sigh. You just got here, and all the adults want to do is eat.

"You can explore a little if you wish," Mom suggests. "We'll be here at the restaurant if you need us."

You head off on your own. You enter the castle grounds through a narrow passageway. The walls are made of cold stone. You walk until you find a room with a door left open. Inside is a wooden table stained with fake blood—probably from the haunted mansion event.

As you turn to leave, someone touches you on the shoulder. You look around, but there's no one here. Did you imagine that?

You head quickly out of the room, but the sound of sobbing stops you. Do you investigate?

- To look for the source of the sobbing, turn to page 58.
- To run out of the room, turn to page 62.

Curious, you turn around. That wooden table with the blood stains now has a body lying on it. Where did it come from?

The body looks as if random body parts have been sewn together. Before you can take a step closer, its eyes open.

Terrified, you run to the courtyard. It is filled with small children in cute costumes. Your cousins run up to you.

"Let's go into the chapel," they say, pulling you by the hand.

They lead you to a small church. Inside, the walls are white. The partially stained-glass windows light up as the sun shines through them. There are candles lit and flowers everywhere. A plaque explains that this is a popular place for weddings.

Your cousins run around the chapel and climb on the benches. You tell them to be careful and not to run in a church. You sit on a bench and admire the small altar with a golden cross placed on top of a white, lace cloth. Someone sits down next to you. It's a bride. She's crying quietly.

You stand up quickly. "Oh! I'm sorry. We didn't realize there was a wedding here today," you say.

You turn to grab your cousins, but they're gone. There's suddenly no one in here but you and the bride. She turns to look at you. Her eyes are ringed with dark circles, and her skin is pale. This can't be real. The bride opens her mouth, and the moan that emerges pierces you to your bones.

Turn the page.

The ghost floats over you with a shriek and flies at the altar. She knocks over the cross. It crashes loudly on the stone floor. Then she flies out through the large window at the back of the chapel.

Your heart is pounding when you hear a small voice say, "I have to go to the bathroom."

You blink several times, as if waking from a bad dream, and look down. Your cousin is standing beside you. You're relieved to have a reason to leave this place.

THE END

To follow another path, turn to page 8.
To learn more about haunted castles, turn to page 103.

You run out of the room as fast as you can. You emerge at the other end of the passageway and enter a small, sunny courtyard. Costumed children run around, happily.

The courtyard is between the castle, a small chapel, and a tower. You decide to check out the tower.

It's a long climb up many flights of stairs. But when you get to the top, the view is amazing. The town below and the forest near the castle look like they're from a fairy tale.

Suddenly, you catch a glimpse of something glowing in the trees. When you look again, it's gone.

Maybe people are camping in the forest, you think.

You head back down. Resting at one of the windows, you look out over the chapel. A man sits on the roof holding a bag. He is dressed in medieval clothing and wears a wig of tightly curled grey hair. He seems upset. He's yelling in German and clearly troubled. You should get someone to help him.

You run to the visitor's desk. A security guard accompanies you back to the courtyard below the chapel, but the man is gone. The guard questions the other tourists in the area, but you're the only person who saw this man.

A shiver runs through you. Did you imagine him? Or did you see an actual ghost?

THE END

To follow another path, turn to page 8.
To learn more about haunted castles, turn to page 103.

You go with the group to the forest. The trees cast long, eerie shadows in the moonlight.

You take a deep breath of cool air and look up toward the tops of the tall trees. When you look back down, the rest of the group is discussing the unusual plants that grow here. You're not interested, so you wander on your own, deeper into the forest.

Through the trees, you spot a small light. You saw it from the tower. There must be campers out there.

You walk toward it as the light grows bigger. It's a large bonfire in a clearing. A ring of men and women dressed in black dance and sing around it. You've never heard this language before.

You watch them, mesmerized. When they're done, they gather near the fire and speak loudly. You wish you understood their language. They seem excited.

A woman in a long gown appears on the other side of the fire. She holds a silver cup over her head. The others cheer. They take turns sipping from the cup.

You step closer, to get a better look. A twig breaks under your foot. Everyone goes quiet. All eyes are on you.

"I'm sorry," you stammer, taking a step back. "I didn't mean to disturb you."

For several seconds, the people stare at you. Are they angry or curious? You take another step back.

Turn the page.

The woman with the cup glides gracefully over to you. She holds out the cup.

"Uh, no thank you," you say. You know better than to accept a drink from a stranger. Who knows what could be in it?

The woman won't take no for an answer. She comes in closer. She smells like an old wooden chest in your grandparents' house. She shoves the cup right up to your chin.

"Drink," she insists.

The animal skulls on her outfit knock against each other. Her dark eyes glare at you. She pushes the cup up to your lips and tilts it. You feel the cool liquid touch your mouth. You must do something.

Without thinking, you turn and run for the trees. Several times, you almost trip on roots sticking up from the ground. You turn back to see if anyone is chasing you.

Bam! You run into someone.

"Ouch!" You recognize Aunt Sharon's voice.

You can't stop apologizing, as you realize you've rejoined your tour group. Sharon rubs her sore nose. When the guide suggests you all move deeper into the woods, you pull Sharon aside.

Turn the page.

"I'm tired" you whisper. "Can we go home?"

Sharon seems relieved. "Of course. The jet leg must have caught up to you."

On the car ride, you wonder if you should tell Sharon what you saw in the forest.

"Aunt Sharon," you say nervously. "Have you ever seen anything strange at Castle Frankenstein."

Sharon gives you a knowing look. "Yes," she says. "And I take it you did too?"

You nod. You don't want to talk about it anymore, but you're relieved Aunt Sharon understands.

THE END

To follow another path, turn to page 8.
To learn more about haunted castles, turn to page 103.

You go with the group to the chapel. Someone says they've been to a wedding here.

"It's very romantic," one girl says.

You wonder how romantic a haunted chapel can be. But when you step inside, you're surprised to see that it's lovely. Candles line the walls and windowsills. There are flowers at the end of each row. At the front, there's a small altar with a cross on it.

You look out through the decorative side window. When you turn back to head out, there's a bride standing there. She's staring at you through a thick veil. You get the feeling she's not happy.

You take a step closer. "Hello," you say.

Her reply is a terrifying shriek. She lifts off the ground and flies right at you.

As she zooms through you, it feels like being hit by a hundred giant spider webs. You wave your arms about, trying to shake off the feeling of cobwebs.

One of the girls you came with lays a hand on you. "Are you all right?" she asks.

You look around as your heart rate slows back to normal.

"Did you see a ghost?" she asks. "I've heard there's an angry bride that haunts this room."

"I . . . I think I did," you say, stunned. You feel rather stupid.

"I'll tell you a secret," the girl says, sitting beside you.

"I think I've heard it," she says. "Once, when I was in here alone, I was sure I heard sobbing and then a scream. But I didn't stay long enough to see anything. I was so scared."

You sigh in relief. You're not the only one who's had this experience. You tell her what you saw. Your new friend drapes her arm around you. You sit in the silence of your common experience.

THE END

To follow another path, turn to page 8.
To learn more about haunted castles, turn to page 103.

CHAPTER 4
THE FORBIDDEN CITY IN BEIJING, CHINA

You choose the school trip to Beijing, China. Ever since you were little, your grandmother has told you ghost stories from her childhood in China. Her favorite ones took place in the Imperial Palace, known as the Forbidden City. They were your favorite too. Because of them, you have always been intrigued by ghosts.

On the third day there, you finally get to visit the Forbidden City. Your group of twenty-five students is met by a tour guide, Ms. Lin. She's petite with long black hair, but she has a loud voice that commands respect.

Turn the page.

At the entrance, Ms. Lin explains that the palace grounds cover 180 acres. There are almost 1,000 buildings and about 9,000 rooms here. Not all of it is open to the public.

She hands you all maps of the grounds. "Over its 600 years of history, there have been many plots, murders, and tragedies," she says. "Many spirits linger."

Your friends, twins Addison and Aiden, make spooky sounds and laugh.

"In China, we take ghosts very seriously," Ms. Lin continues, looking at the twins. "Even the wise philosopher Confucius said, 'Respect the ghosts and gods, but keep away from them.'"

She leads your group across the enormous stone courtyard and stops at the bottom of some steps leading up to a giant door.

On each side of the gate sits a tall statue of a creature. They look like something between a lion and a dog.

"You'll see these gatekeepers. They guard most of the doorways in the palace," Ms. Lin says. "Their job is to keep the evil spirits away."

Ms. Lin says you may follow her for a guided tour or wander the grounds and buildings on your own. "Your map booklets have explanations to help you understand what you're looking at."

- To stay with Ms. Lin, turn to page 76.
- To explore the palace on your own, turn to page 87.

You feel like you'll learn more with the tour guide. About half the group stays with her, including the twins. You climb up the stairs and enter the Hall of Supreme Harmony.

"This is the most important building in the palace," Ms. Lin says. "It is very sacred."

You almost trip over the high step at the doorway. Ms. Lin looks concerned.

"Every doorway in the palace has a step like that," she says. "Ghosts cannot jump, so these high steps are meant to keep them from leaving the rooms that they haunt."

Your group stands at the bottom of what looks like a large altar. Ms. Lin goes on for a while about the history here. But you're distracted by the Chinese flute music in the background.

You break off from the group to look for the musician.

"Excuse me," Ms. Lin calls to you. "Please stay with the group."

You ask her about the music. Her brows furrow. "What music?" she asks.

No one else seems to have heard it either. You shake it off and continue with the tour.

As you walk past rooms and small courtyards, Ms. Lin explains that over one million laborers were used to build the Forbidden City. It took only 14 years.

"They used blocks that click together," she says.

"Like building blocks?" Aiden asks.

You don't hear her answer because an adorable black and white cat runs past you. You try to point it out to your friends, but they're listening to the guide. You're curious as to where the cat went. Do you follow it?

- To continue on the tour, go to page 79.
- To follow the cat, turn to page 84.

Addison pulls you along with her as she tries to stay at the front of the group. You all walk through a small courtyard and a series of rooms. Beautiful carvings decorate the rooms.

As your group leaves one room, you are distracted by lights hanging off the ceiling. There aren't any wires or handles on these lights. They simply float in midair.

"How do the lights do that?" you ask Ms. Lin.

The guide doesn't answer. She looks at you as if you'd just come from outer space.

"What lights?" she asks.

When you try to show her, the lights are gone. You are bewildered, and Ms. Lin looks scared.

"Do you also see mist in the rooms?" she asks.

"Only in two of them," you reply. "I thought you did that for effect."

"I don't see anything," Addison says, giving you a funny look.

Ms. Lin mumbles something in Chinese. You only catch one word that grandma has taught you—*gui*. It means "ghost."

The group continues on to another side of the Forbidden City. It's the Eastern Glorious Gate, that is also called the Ghost Gate.

"The ghost of the last emperor of the Ming dynasty haunts this place," Ms. Lin says. "His body was put on display here, and he wasn't happy about it. His spirit hasn't been able to leave."

"Do you see his ghost?" Addison teases.

Turn the page.

The Eastern Glorious Gate of the Forbidden City

"No," you say. You like the paranormal, but you hate being teased.

Just then, you catch a blurred image out of the corner of your eye. You don't want your classmates to notice you see something. You turn casually in that direction and see a man in a white robe flitting across the courtyard.

You move a little closer toward the man. He whips around to face you. That's when you see that his head hangs at an odd angle, as if his neck is broken. You yelp in fright.

"Now what?" Aiden asks, laughing.

Everyone is staring at you. Ms. Lin's face has gone white.

You take a deep breath as your heart rate slows back down.

"Sorry," you say. "I . . . uh . . . tripped."

Ms. Lin looks like she can tell you're lying. She moves through the rest of the tour at a quicker pace. She seems distracted and never makes eye contact with you again.

You wonder if all of grandma's stories have you imagining things. Or are they real?

THE END

To follow another path, turn to page 8.
To learn more about haunted castles, turn to page 103.

Your group heads over to a long wall with nine dragons carved into it. As beautiful as it is, you follow the cat down a narrow passageway.

"Here kitty!" you call.

The passageway leads to another misty courtyard. The cat appears out of the mist. She meows at you and walks between your legs. You reach out to pet her, but your hand goes right through her.

What is this? The cat saunters away and disappears into the mist. At that moment, the sound of clashing metal fills the air. It sounds like sword fighting.

You walk through the mist, searching for the fighters. You'd love to watch a demonstration of this ancient martial art form.

At the other end of the courtyard, you see shadows of two people clashing swords with loud clangs. You look around and wonder why no other tourists are here to watch this show. But when you try to get a closer look, there's no one there. Your heart thumps wildly.

You break into a run and head back toward your group. Ms. Lin is just finishing up the tour. No one seems to have noticed that you were missing. Ms. Lin leads you all back to where you began the trip.

"Is the tour over?" you ask Addison.

"Yes, finally," Aiden says. "Three hours is as long as I can stand."

"It was interesting," Addison adds, "But I was hoping to see some ghosts."

Turn the page.

You wish you could say the same. Three hours? You were gone for that long? A cold shiver runs through you. It didn't feel like you were gone long at all.

You can't wait to get out of here. Grandma's ghost stories might have intrigued you, but in real life, they're terrifying.

THE END

To follow another path, turn to page 8.
To learn more about haunted castles, turn to page 103.

You turn to the twins. "Will you come with me to explore on our own?" you ask.

"Sure," Aiden says. "The big group will move too slowly, anyway."

"Yeah," adds Addison, waving her map. "I can be our tour guide."

With maps in hand, you and the twins head off on your own. You walk through several courtyards that are surrounded by smaller rooms. Addison reads aloud from the booklet.

"From the 1400s to the 1900s, emperors would have many wives," she reads. "Some would only see their husband once in their entire life. The women created their own communities in these smaller courtyards."

Turn the page.

You admire the beautifully carved wood furniture in one of the rooms. Out of the corner of your eye, you see a woman sitting on a bed in the next room with her face in her hands. She's dressed in a white gown and sobbing.

"Are you okay?" you ask.

She looks up at you, surprised. Her face is a pale green, and her eyes are large and dark. She opens her mouth and lets out a blood-curdling scream.

You jump back and trip over the step at the doorway. Landing on your bottom, you look up at the woman. She's floating over you, shrieking. She looks angry. You crab-crawl backward until you're outside the room. The ghost seems stuck behind the threshold.

"Why are you on the floor?" Addison appears at your side. You try to answer her, but you can't catch your breath. As Aiden helps you to your feet, Addison tells you what she's read about this part of the palace.

"In 1421, Emperor Yongle's favorite wife died," she says. "He claimed one of his other wives or romantic partners must have poisoned her, so he had 2,800 of them killed."

You are horrified at the thought of such a mass murder. You wonder if that ghost was one of those ladies.

Addison reads on. "Sixteen of his wives weren't in the palace that day. Their lives were spared. But when he died, they were hanged right here in this courtyard."

Turn the page.

"But before the emperor died, there was a terrible fire that burned 250 buildings and killed a lot of people. The emperor believed he was cursed for killing all those ladies." Addison closes her booklet.

"Wow, that's a lot of dead people," Aiden says. "I wonder if their ghosts are still around."

You don't want to tell him that you may have just seen one. Just then, two of the largest dogs you've ever seen trot past the end of the courtyard. They're muscular, with fluffy coats, and are at least half your height.

"Did you see those huge dogs?"

"Dogs? Where?" Addison gasps. "Let's go find them."

You point in the direction you saw them run. Just then, you hear a woman singing in Chinese.

"Sounds like there's a stage show happening somewhere," you say, as the music stops suddenly. "That was a pretty song."

The twins stare at you. "What song?"

You gulp. Maybe it's safer to chase after the dogs. At least they're real. But you swear the singing is too. Maybe the twins just weren't paying attention.

What do you do?

- To follow the large dogs, go to page 92.
- To find the singer, turn to page 98.

"They went this way," you tell Addison and Aiden. You point in the direction they ran off.

Neither of the twins saw them, but they follow you without question. You follow the dogs through several passageways. They turn left and right down many paths, between buildings.

When you are out of breath, you stop in a small garden to rest for a moment. The twins are panting as well.

Addison flips through her booklet to learn where you are. "Oh no," she says. "This is one of the areas closed to the public."

You search the garden, but there's no sign of the dogs. Disappointed, you tell your friends you should find a way back.

That's when you hear the snarling. You freeze. "Do you hear that?" you ask the twins.

The look of fright on their faces tells you they do. Two large dogs stand in front of you. Their bodies vibrate with a low, ferocious growl. Their lips are curled back to reveal sharp, white fangs.

"What do we do?" Aiden whispers.

- To run, turn to page 94.
- To stand still, turn to page 96.

"Run!" you cry.

All three of you turn and run. You swear you hear the dogs behind you. You dart out of the courtyard and past several buildings. Still, the sounds of barking and panting follow you. Finally, you are all out of breath.

"I can't run anymore," Addison cries.

You look back at her and see that the dogs are gone.

"It's okay," you say. "They're gone."

All three of you are confused and scared.

"What the heck happened?" Aiden asks.

"I don't know," you say. "But I'm ready to get out of this place.

A building in the courtyard of the Forbidden City

THE END

To follow another path, turn to page 8.
To learn more about haunted castles, turn to page 103.

"Don't move," you say.

"And then what?" Addison says.

Before you come up with an answer, the bigger dog lunges at you. Addison screams, and you hold your breath. There's nothing you can do to save yourself. You cross your arms over your face and wait for the pain.

But it never comes. When you open your eyes, the dogs are gone.

"What happened?" Aiden asks, breathless.

You look around. There's no sign of the dogs at all.

"Could they have been ghosts?" Addison asks.

All three of you stand in silence for several minutes. You're shaking in fear.

"Let's get out of here," Aiden suggests. You agree.

Following the map, you make your way out to the entrance meeting point. You are relieved when you find yourselves outside the Forbidden City once again. This experience was so spooky that you and the twins just sit at a bottom step and say nothing until your classmates appear.

"Let's not say anything to anyone," Addison whispers to you as your teacher appears.

"They'd never believe us anyway," Aiden adds.

You agree. You don't think anyone would ever believe what happened—not even Grandma.

THE END

To follow another path, turn to page 8.
To learn more about haunted castles, turn to page 103.

"Listen. They're playing the song again," you say. "It sounds like they're preparing to perform."

The twins pause to listen. They don't hear it.

The singer's voice is distant but pretty. You don't understand the words, but its sad notes call to you. You run down several pathways until you come to a small garden. There are flowers blooming everywhere. Tall trees, heavy with fruit, give you shade from the hot sun.

"This is a happy place," Addison says. You agree, but you're puzzled why you're still the only one who can hear the music.

Each of you wanders off to a different corner of the garden. You're admiring some red flowers when suddenly the temperature drops. Is a ghost nearby?

You look around and see three women in flowing blue gowns floating amongst the trees. They don't seem bothered by your presence. You watch in awe as they float from tree to tree.

One of the women reaches up to touch a fruit. She's singing the song you've been hearing.

You should be terrified, but the scene is strangely peaceful. You sit on a stone bench and enjoy the supernatural music.

When the song ends, something dark whips past you. The three ladies have vanished. In their place is a lady in a flowing red gown. Her face is covered behind a red veil. You remember Grandma telling you that Chinese brides wore red and covered their faces before the wedding. Could this be the ghost of a bride who died on her wedding day?

Turn the page.

As you step closer, she rises into the air. She lets out an angry shriek and the veil lifts off until you see that she has no face!

You step back a little too quickly and trip over the stone bench. The fall feels like it happens in slow motion. When your head hits the ground, pain zings through your body. Just before you black out, the red ghost lady flies over you, laughing.

When you wake up, your schoolmates are staring down at you.

"What happened?" several people ask.

Even Addison and Aiden have no explanation. "One minute she was sitting on the bench, the next, she's lying on the ground," Aiden tells Ms. Lin.

Ms. Lin leans in close. "Did you see a ghost?"

You nod slowly. Ms. Lin smiles. "I knew there was something special about you."

As you rub the sore spot on the back of your head, you're not sure you agree with the tour guide. You don't feel special. The experience was terrifying. You can't wait to get home to tell Grandma. She might be the only one to understand.

As you walk away from the Forbidden City, a strange sadness fills you. So many tortured spirits live there still. You wish you'd known how to help them.

THE END

To follow another path, turn to page 8.
To learn more about haunted castles, turn to page 103.

CHAPTER 5
ARE CASTLE HAUNTINGS REAL?

Stories of ghost dogs running around the Forbidden City are not uncommon. People driving past Leap Castle in Ireland often see light coming from the window of the Bloody Chapel. They believe that the priest who was killed there is still upset at being murdered by his brother. The sound of rattling bones coming from the roof of the chapel in Castle Frankenstein has been heard by several visitors. So, are ghosts real?

Scientists often have explanations for some of these experiences. A sudden drop in temperature could be a draft from a window or a chimney. Low humidity can also create this feeling of cold.

Experiments have shown that very low-frequency sound waves can also cause people to see things that aren't there. These waves are so quiet that our ears can't hear them, but the waves can affect our eyes. Scientists think that simply because people want to see ghosts, they can be persuaded that they're real.

Many scientists insist that ghosts don't exist. But some experiences are difficult to explain. Do you think there is always a scientific explanation, or do you believe in ghosts?

Whether you believe in ghosts or not, the histories of castles are long and often tortured. They capture the human imagination with their bloody pasts and spooky mysteries.

MORE GHOSTLY ENCOUNTERS

Castles all over the world have famous and spooky histories. Bran Castle in Romania is known as Dracula's castle. Bram Stoker wrote the book *Dracula* and named his main character after Vlad the Impaler. This nobleman lived in Romania in the 1400's. He was a cruel and vicious fighter who tortured his enemies to death. He may have lived at this castle at one point. Ghost hunters have come here, hoping to see his ghost.

Bran Castle, Transylvania, Romania

The Tower of London is also said to be a haunted castle. Many people were executed there, including Anne Boleyn, one of the six wives of King Henry the Eighth. Others were imprisoned in this tower. The scariest ghost here is the phantom bear. It is said one guard died of fright from seeing this specter.

Himeji Castle in Japan has a ghost that is said to have risen from a well into which she was thrown. She is known to count to nine and then scream. The story is that she was a servant at this castle. Her Lord had ten favorite plates, and it was her job to keep them safe. When a samurai fell in love with her, she rejected him, so he hid one of the plates. The samurai told her he'd return the tenth plate if she married him, but she refused. So, he threw her in the well. Her ghost came back to look for that last plate.

OTHER PATHS TO EXPLORE

Imagine you lived in a location that was rumored to be haunted. How would you feel about strangers coming to your house as tourists? Would you welcome them in, or would it feel like they were invading your privacy?

Imagine you were a ghost hunter who wanted to prove the existence of ghosts scientifically. What kind of experiments would you set up to prove it? What results do you think would prove ghosts are real and why?

Let's say ghosts are real, and you're a ghost. What kinds of life experiences would cause your spirit to get stuck on Earth? How might the living help you move on?

GLOSSARY

chieftain (CHEEF-tuhn)—a leader of a clan or tribe

clan (KLAN)—a group of people related by a common ancestor

earl (UHRL)—a rich and powerful English man

electromagnetic field (i-lek-troh-mag-NET-ik FEELD)—a field of force created by moving electric charges

humidity (hyoo-MIH-du-tee)—the measure of the moisture in the air

legend (LEJ-uhnd)—a story passed down through the years that may not be completely true

mass (MASS)—a Catholic worship service

spirit (SPIHR-it)—the invisible part of a person that contains thoughts and feelings; some people believe the spirit leaves the body after death

torture (TOR-chuhr)—to cause intense pain or suffering

BIBLIOGRAPHY

The Forbidden City: Highlights, Secret of the Name, Facts
chinahighlights.com/beijing/forbidden-city/

Frankenstein Castle
germany-insider-facts.com/frankenstein-castle.html

Henderson, Jan-Andrew. *The Ghost that Haunted Itself: The Story of the McKenzie Poltergeist.* Edinburgh: Mainstream, 2001.

How Ghosts Work
science.howstuffworks.com/science-vs-myth/afterlife/ghost3.htm

Leap Castle
leapcastle.net/?page_id=36

The Top Three Scientific Explanations for Ghost Sightings
theconversation.com/the-top-three-scientific-explanations-for-ghost-sightings-58259

This Is The Most Haunted Castle In Ireland
theirishroadtrip.com/most-haunted-castle-in-ireland/

READ MORE

Gottschall, Meghan. *Haunts and Horrors.* Fremont, CA: Full Tilt Press, 2019.

Kempster, Rachel. *The Ghostly Tales of Long Island.* Charleston, SC: Arcadia Children's Books, a division of Arcadia Publishing, 2020.

Peterson, Megan Cooley. *Can You Escape a Haunted Battlefield?: An Interactive Paranormal Adventure.* North Mankato, MN: Capstone, 2025.

INTERNET SITES

The Forbidden City—A Nest of Ghost Stories
bizarreglobehopper.com/blog/2016/03/29/forbidden-city-ghost-stories/

Frankenstein Castle: Legends, Myths & Spectacular Halloween Parties
germany-insider-facts.com/frankenstein-castle.html

Leap Castle: The Hauntings
leapcastle.net/?page_id=36

ABOUT THE AUTHOR

Ailynn Collins learned a lot about writing from her teachers at Hamline University in St. Paul, MN. She has always loved reading science fiction stories about other worlds and strange aliens. She enjoys creating new characters and worlds for her stories, as well as envisioning what the future might look like. When not writing, Collins enjoys spending her spare time reading and playing board games with her family. She lives near Seattle, Washington, with her husband and lovable dogs.